THE PROMISE OF DIGITAL GOVERNMENT: TRANSFORMING PUBLIC SERVICES, REGULATION, AND CITIZENSHIP

Menzies Research Centre
March, 2016

Published in 2016 by Connor Court Publishing Pty Ltd

Connor Court Publishing Pty Ltd.
PO Box 7257
Redland Bay QLD 4165
sales@connorcourt.com
www.connorcourt.com
Phone 0497 900 685

ISBN: 978-1-925501-02-5

Cover design, Ian James

Printed in Australia

"When a nation gives up pioneering, it goes back. A pioneer is, quite simply, one who breaks new ground or sets out on new adventures. In a slave community, the only great enterprise is despotic government itself. It is in free communities that the citizen gets his chance."

--Sir Robert Menzies, 1954[1]

FOREWORD

Robert Menzies spoke of Australians as a pioneering people; Malcolm Turnbull speaks of a nation of innovators. The rhetoric may be different, but their prime ministerial message is similar: the source of Australia's future prosperity will be the ingenuity, enterprise and industry of its citizens.

As Angus Taylor writes in this incisive essay, digital disruption is transforming our lives in ways we could not have imagined. Businesses are operating more effectively and efficiently and customers, for the most part, have never been happier thanks to the choice, convenience and value the digital world provides.

Yet while the private sector delivers countless new products and services that make our lives easier, governments appear less agile, locked into traditional processes that seem increasingly slow and unresponsive. Businesses such as banks that have invested heavily in consumer-focused technology have experienced sharp increases in customer satisfaction. Satisfaction with governments and the services they provide, on the other hand, is generally declining.

When Prime Minister Malcolm Turnbull released his innovation statement late last year, he pledged that the Government would lead by example. The business of government must be digitally transformed to make dealing with government as easy as dealing with eBay. There was no reason, he said, why most transactions with government could not be conducted on smartphones.

In *The Promise of Digital Government* Taylor charts a course to fulfill that pledge and, in the process, deliver leaner, more cost-effective services to

Australians. The essay carries a powerful subtext: digital technology puts the customers in charge. Disruption can help restore the balance between the state and the individual; government services will become customer-focused; government's direction will be driven less by bureaucrats and more by the wisdom of crowds; government are likely to become more transparent and accountable; government departments can morph from being data hoarders into data providers, offering open-source information that will fuel innovation in the private sector.

Digital technology releases the power of Adam Smith's invisible hand and vindicates Friedrich Hayek's belief in the power of democratised knowledge. This e-driven transformation could make much government regulation redundant. In the era of Uber and the sharing economy, customers are empowered; companies that wish to survive need to meet customers' needs, including for convenience and security, allowing markets to largely regulate themselves.

Of course, we should expect resistance. The digital revolution is the enemy of top-down, centralised government, and those with vested interests in maintaining the status quo will fight back. We need firm leadership and relentless focus if digitisation is to achieve its potential in the public sector.

The good news is that digital innovation has a momentum that is difficult to resist in a liberal, democratic and inventive country such as ours. In countless, subversive and exciting ways it puts the individual back in charge. With the right political leadership, digital disruption will create the kind of nation to which Menzies aspired, where progress is driven not by government departments but by the creative genius of its citizens.

-- Nick Cater
Executive Director, Menzies Research Centre, March 2016

The Author

Angus Taylor was elected to Federal parliament in September 2013. The boundaries of his NSW seat of Hume were re-drawn (2016) to include some of the fastest growing population areas in southwest Sydney.

With a strong interest in economics, Angus initially worked at a parliamentary committee level on reforming health, tax and agricultural policy and on telecommunications infrastructure.

In February 2016 he was appointed Assistant Minister to the Prime Minister with special responsibility for Cities and Digital Transformation.

Angus is keen for government to implement innovative deals with the private sector, which move more jobs closer to where people live and ensure a strong return for taxpayer dollars invested.

He is a firm believer in government delivering more effective public services through digitisation.

Prior to entering parliament in 2013, Angus was a Director at Port Jackson Partners where he was a strategy and business advisor to a number of global and Australian companies, as well as public sector organisations. Before this he was a partner at global consulting firm McKinsey & Co.

Angus has a Bachelor of Economics (First Class Honours and University Medal) and a Bachelor of Laws (Honours) from the University of Sydney. He also has a Master of Philosophy in Economics from the University of

Oxford, where he studied as a Rhodes Scholar. His thesis was in the field of competition policy.

In his private capacity Angus has founded and advised a number of small, fast growing start-up businesses. He has co-authored in depth economic analyses including *Earth, Fire, Wind and Water – Economic Opportunity and the Australian Commodities Cycle* (2011) and *Greener Pastures – The Soft Commodity Opportunity for Australia and New Zealand* (2012).

TABLE OF CONTENTS

1

INTRODUCTION

- Citizens are demanding more with less but governments around the world are failing to meet expectations
- Increasingly, government is a data driven organisation – similar to banks and retailers
- Broad-reaching digitisation of government is an enormous opportunity to deliver more with less
  - o Technology offers the potential to substantially reduce costs and offer new and improved government services in ways that were never anticipated
  - o Empowered consumers and citizens can achieve for reform what traditional political processes cannot
- Australian governments need to catch up urgently with accelerated strategic investment of effort and resources

In October 2013 the Obama regime launched the centrepiece of its new healthcare program. The website, *healthcare.gov*, had cost hundreds of millions of dollars to build and was heralded as a hub that would offer seamless access to health insurance. Immediately after launch, however, the site started crashing. Users found themselves waiting so long that the site was essentially unusable and quickly became the butt of television talk show jokes.

"When you type in your age, it's not clear if they want the age you are right now, or the age you'll be when you finally log in" mocked Jay Leno. President Obama had no choice but to take it on the chin. "There's no sugar coating: the website has been too slow," he said, "and I think it's fair to say that nobody's more frustrated by that than I am."

Much has been written on the causes of the crashes, but central to the problem was the need to screen individual users according to their eligibility for healthcare subsidies so they would only see personalised prices. It meant verifying the identity of the user by linking to a range of different government databases. The ability to break down silos across government and provide an integrated customised picture for consumers or citizens is one of the key challenges to digitising government services, but it had failed its first serious test.[2]

The failure was a political and public relations disaster for the Obama administration which had worked hard to build support for its controversial healthcare scheme. The signing of the *Patient Protection and Affordable Care Act* was the culmination of many years of negotiation with myriad interest groups, Congress and the Senate. The launch of *healthcare.gov* was to have been a symbol demonstrating that the scheme was up and running. Some of America's top government officials had been deployed to work on the project and little expense had been spared in commissioning respected IT experts. So what had gone wrong and who was responsible?

An investigation by the Government Accountability Office attributed the blame almost entirely to the administration. Bureaucrats had failed to give contractors a coherent plan and forced them to work within compressed time frames. Bureaucrats kept changing the contractors' marching orders creating confusion and adding tens of millions of dollars to the cost. Oversight procedures had been poor and lines of responsibility blurred.[3] Even before the disastrous launch, an expert complained "the political people in the administration do not understand how far behind they are."[4]

The consequences of the crash echoed around the world. Digital failure had led to a political and policy disaster. The digitisation of services was regarded as the key to running an effective, modern government. The high-stakes failure of *healthcare.gov* cast serious doubt on the ability of governments to make progress.

The problem we need to solve

The embrace of digital technology by the private sector has changed much of our lives for the better, increasing choice, speed, productivity and consumer satisfaction. By comparison governments appear clunky and unresponsive. It is little wonder that voters throughout the developed world are increasingly cynical about government. Expectations are high, but delivery is low and containment of spending growth seems like a pipedream. Citizens are disengaged, cynical and fickle.

We shouldn't be surprised. The private sector has spoilt consumers for choice, innovation, and downward pressure on prices. Apple has reshaped communications and music, Facebook social interactions, Ikea furniture and Aldi retail, just to name a few. In almost every category of goods and services we get far better value than only a few years ago. Customers have become brutal and ruthless in choosing products and services at the prices they want. They share information on their experiences and they learn quickly from each other.

Not so for public services. Choice is limited, costs blow out and the customer isn't in charge. Politicians who promise more with less are treated with scepticism and understandably so. Citizens are conditioned to governments failing to deliver and spending more money in a vain attempt to fix the problem. If you want more from government, you need more money allocated to your cause. Innovation is rarely in the mix.

Public service innovation and productivity goes missing

In economic terms, the fundamental problem is a lack of productivity improvement in the provision of public services. Whether it is health, education, employment services or transport infrastructure – governments simply haven't put enough emphasis on rapid improvement in the quality and cost of public services. These challenges will only get tougher. Rapid ageing of the population will put enormous pressure on budgets[5], as older populations work less and require more spending on health, welfare and aged care.

Meanwhile, pressure from unions and other vested interests is stymying labour productivity gains. Governments have given in to demands to fix or increase staffing ratios, such as the number of teachers per student and have ignored research or innovations that point in the opposite direction. So bad is the situation that even conservative policy leaders, who previously focused on lower taxes and spending, have started talking about higher taxes and spending.[6]

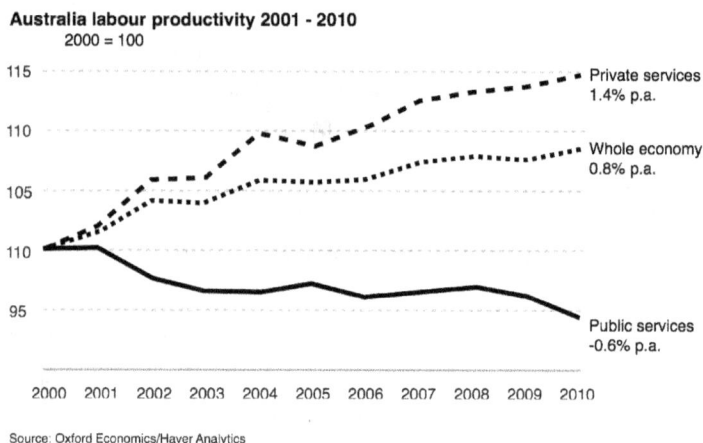

Australia labour productivity 2001 - 2010
2000 = 100

115		Private services 1.4% p.a.
110		
105		Whole economy 0.8% p.a.
110		
95		Public services -0.6% p.a.

2000 2001 2002 2003 2004 2005 2006 2007 2008 2009 2010

Source: Oxford Economics/Haver Analytics

Figure 1: Public sector productivity languishes

In the seminal book, *The Rise and Decline of Nations*, Mancur Olsen observed that vested interests block structural change[7], threatening the very foundations on which successful civilisations are built. Increasingly, western democracies are struggling to get beyond vested interests to mainstream interests, to deliver innovation and productivity gains in the provision of public services. The left thinks that business interests are getting undue control of the political process. The right thinks unions, NGOs and left wing activists look to create jobs for themselves on the back of 'do-gooder' environmental, social and political objectives. Neither side argues with any conviction that mainstream interests are well represented.

Historically, a number of economists have argued that services don't lend themselves to productivity gains, calling this problem Baumol's cost disease. A study of the American performing arts sector in the 1960s by William J. Baumol and William G. Bowen had argued that it took the same number of musicians to play a Beethoven string quartet today as it did in the 19th century. Yet the study ignored the many other productivity gains that innovation offers. We can now listen to an orchestra on our iPhones at any time of the day or night with no musicians present, a breakthrough that like the gramophone before it, offers a substantial reduction in the ratio between the number of musicians and the size of the audience.

Even the left wing economist JK Galbraith highlighted the relative failure of delivery on public versus private services, contrasting "private affluence" with "public squalor."

> We worry about our schools. We worry about our public recreational facilities. We worry about our law enforcement and our public housing. All of the things that bear upon our standard of living are in the public sector. We don't worry about the supply of automobiles. We don't even worry about the supply of foods. Things that come from the private sector are in abundant supply; things that depend on the public sector are widely a problem.[8]

Galbraith wrongly claimed that the problem was insufficient spending on public goods relative to private investment. In fact the failure of the public sector to spend money efficiently and effectively is the bigger culprit.[9]

Not only is the public sector failing to recognise the growing power of consumers, it is failing to recognise the growing power of citizenship. Citizenship was once characterised by a strong sense of duty and high levels of participation in volunteer organisations. There is reason to believe that many citizens are as enthusiastic about participation as they ever were, but the opportunity costs for busy two income families with large mortgages are high. As we shall see, simple, quick ways to participate in local communities are welcomed by many citizens.

Australia's starting point in delivering public service is not hopeless. In some areas, Australia is already a world leader. Our health system fares reasonably well, and until recently our education performed well too. We have a tax and welfare system that is progressive and well targeted compared to others. The problem is more about the future than the past. In recent years, the dials have all started moving in the wrong direction and change is desperately needed.

So what's the answer?

The rapid evolution of information technologies offers the potential to give power back to customers and citizens and away from inflexible governments and their chosen providers. We have already seen this happening in the private sector; the public sector now needs to play catch up. Customers of our public schools, health system and welfare system – even 'customers' of our taxation system – can be empowered like never before through web technologies. This will challenge vested interests and providers to focus more on customers and less on themselves.

There is, unfortunately, increasing cynicism about the ability of the political class to drive reforms to solve this problem.[10] Political parties are fragmenting in many countries as small parties gain momentum, and media polarisation is rewarding populism on both the left and right. Legislative deadlock is endemic. The interests and views of mainstream voters are not cutting through.

All of this at a time when technology offers to radically transform delivery of public services – education, health, welfare, justice, infrastructure, national security and tax collection. At no time in the history of government have we been in a better position to deliver improved services in all of these areas, and technology is at the heart of the opportunity.

The promise of digital government

Two very simple ideas are central to this monograph.

First, technology offers the potential for substantially reduced costs alongside improved and better targeted government services. Disruption in the delivery of an increasingly complex array of government services is now possible in ways that were never previously anticipated. In defence, health, education, policing or food labelling, every aspect of government needs to be re-examined with an eye to what can and should be done differently to reduce costs and improve services.

Second, empowered consumers and citizens can drive reform in ways that traditional political processes can't, particularly as we increase competition and contestability in the provision of services like aged care and disability. If public sector unions want to block innovations that voters understand and want, voters can apply political pressure. When vested interests get in the way of sensible reforms, transparency will help to shed light on their undue influence. Not only can we disrupt traditional lacklustre public service delivery, but we can redefine regulation and how citizens and customers regulate services for themselves.

These two powerful ideas put the citizen or the customer back at the centre of the work of the modern state, in line with fundamental liberal and conservative principles. Government has become a self-serving beast, and digital technology offers the potential to tame government and refocus it for the benefit of all. Many conservatives and traditional small government liberals have given up on the idea of smaller more effective government which empowers citizens to realise their own aspirations. Efficient government sharply focused on customers and citizens can make a major contribution to reasserting this possibility.

A great deal of work has been done in this area in recent years, but the results are still limited. At the federal level, the Government 2.0 initiative, AGIMO, the Digital Transformation Office and Govhack have all focused on dealing with aspects of this problem. Similar initiatives can be found within state governments.

That past work doesn't need to be replicated, but we desperately need a clearer, more strategic and more focused picture of what is possible, and how we get there. This monograph doesn't set out to provide a detailed blueprint of everything that has to be done to achieve digital nirvana. In fact, much is not knowable. We do need a strategic focus on how we can infuse digital thinking into our most important reforms in every part of government and beyond. We need to see more clearly the potential to deliver more with less, at a time when reform seems beyond reach.

This work is focused on the potential of digital government across all levels of Australian government. We can only realise digital technology's full potential if it reaches all tiers of government, and all areas of government. However, the primary focus is on the Federal Government given its dominant role in modern Australia.

Digital technology offers the promise of containing growth in spending, vastly improved services and genuine reform. It is time for Australian governments to step up and embrace this extraordinary opportunity.

2

BIG DATA, BIG BENEFITS AND BIG SAVINGS

- Digitising all interactions with government and encouraging strong growth of digital channels should be a top priority for all Australian governments
- While direct benefits and savings will be large, they extend well beyond efficiencies and improved services
- Tens of billions of dollars of wasted spending can be eliminated through better compliance and targeting of payments and programmes
  - o Short term savings are achievable by eliminating fraud, abuse and errors ('compliance') in high spending portfolios like health, welfare, taxation and disability
  - o A clear, integrated and granular picture of the impact of current programmes will enable retargeting of expenditure across government

As a new Member of Parliament in 2013, I was immediately struck by the demands on my electorate office. I was fully expecting to deal with a long list of policy issues and political feedback. While that is an important part of my work, I found myself running a customer call centre for a range of government services from telecommunications, to welfare, immigration, health, law and order and education. State and local issues featured just as much as federal issues.

Constituents don't want to be lectured about the three tiers of government, the separation of powers or even the separation between public and private sector. They just want solutions to their problems. Frustrated by endless calls to Indian call centres requiring repeated descriptions of their problem, the bar is not high and solutions are extremely well received. So much so that when a local member is proactive, word gets around that you can solve problems, and the flow of calls and emails increases sharply.

In an attempt to find easier ways to engage with government, a growing number of Australians are attempting to pay their tax online, engage with Centrelink or Medicare online or deal with employment service agencies. In many cases, initial attempts end in frustration. Many keep trying, simply because the alternatives are worse. Call centres with long wait times,[11] or long queues in distant government offices are so infuriating that turning to the web is the only realistic alternative.

Often, the frustrations result in contact with a local member of parliament in the vain hope that they will have a solution to the problem. At least the queue is shorter and there is a genuine welcome, if only because voters matter more to politicians than to bureaucrats. Unfortunately, the local member often lacks the systems and the know-how to solve the most difficult problem, and the constituents' complaint ends up in a ministerial office, before being foisted back into the bureaucracy for more carefully considered inaction.

Whilst my interaction with constituents was welcome, it struck me that much of what governments do could be done much more efficiently and effectively. I began thinking about how much time and money Federal government agencies like Centrelink were wasting because of appalling systems.

While digital government has the potential to profoundly reshape so much of what government does, in the short term its greatest benefits will be in driving savings and improving services for customers, citizens and businesses.

Part of the problem here is the sheer breadth and complexity of the role of modern governments. The twentieth century saw government's role extending well beyond its previous focus on providing a safe and secure environment for citizens to live their own lives and pursue their own interests. Provision of law and order came first. The subsequent growth of the welfare state has been rapid and stunning.

With government taxation below 5% at the beginning of the twentieth century, it is now over 30% across all levels of government and spending is even higher. Those aggregate figures are like the visible tip of the iceberg, as governments have taken on more and more activities, including sharp increases in education and health funding, pensions and a myriad of other welfare payments.

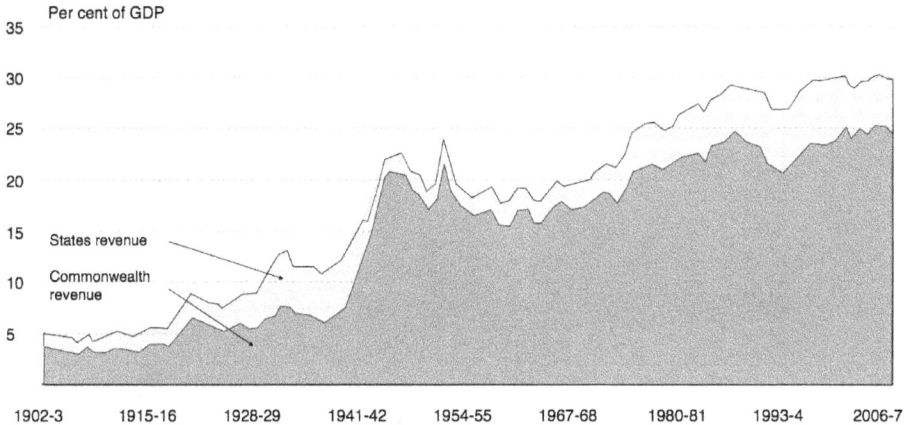

Figure 2: Australian government and state taxation (1902-03 to 2006-07)

As bigger governments have taken on more responsibilities, expectations have increased encouraged by politicians eager to please voters. Governments have typically failed to meet these expectations. The opportunity to streamline engagement with government is enormous, and significant benefits will follow.

It would be easy to fall into the trap of thinking this is a bigger issue for State and even local governments than federal government, given State governments focus on direct provision of services like health, education and vehicle and driver registration and licensing. The facts suggest otherwise. The Federal government has significantly more contact with Australians (45%) versus State and territory (23%) and local government (28%).[12] Much of this Commonwealth Government's contact is driven by tax, welfare, medicare and immigration related issues.

Digitising interactions with government

The shift to digital in the provision of private sector services has been rapid, and customers like it. Around 75% of Australian bank transactions are now done online or through mobile devices.[13] This is amongst the highest in the world and up from almost zero 15 years ago.[14] Despite massive branch closures and constant 'bank bashing', satisfaction levels with banks are now the highest on record.[15] Much of this is being aided by high levels of internet connectivity in Australia, even if it isn't as fast as many would like (see Chapter 6 below).

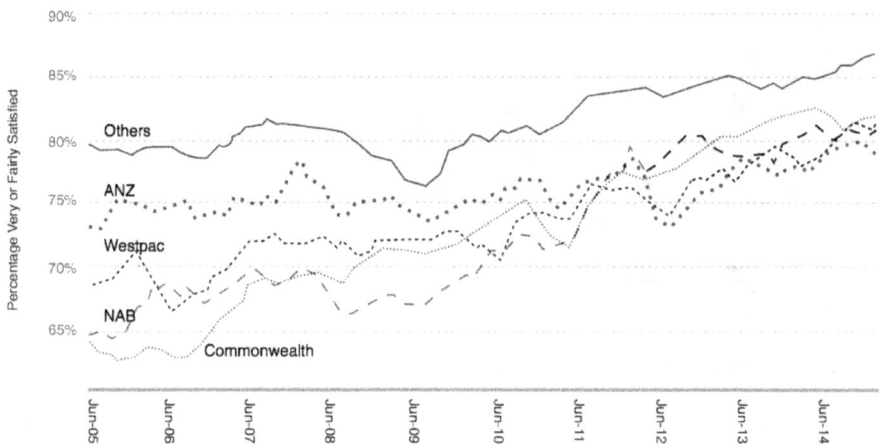

Figure 3: Australian banking customer satisfaction – 2005 to 2015 (Source: Roy Morgan Research)

Meanwhile, banks have reduced costs substantially, passing a large portion of the savings through to customers via low interest margins on loans and deposits. Since 1987, banks net interest margins (the margins they make on loans and deposits) has fallen from 5% to around 2%, with cost to income ratios also falling sharply.[16]

Similar patterns have emerged in travel, insurance, music, media and books. In the airline industry, for instance, over 75% of travellers coming to Australia now plan their trips online and roughly half purchase online, according to Tourism Australia. Even for product sales, we are seeing rapid growth in digital interactions and transactions. Woolworths claims that 83%

of Australians are now regularly using self-scanners in its supermarkets.[17]

The equivalent performance in the public sector would mean high levels of satisfaction with government, lower taxes and better services. This has not been the case. Government already has a great deal of information about each of us, most of which is not currently used in any interaction. The private sector could only wish for this level of knowledge as a starting point.

This is all the more remarkable when we consider that governments' role is focused on services, information sharing and consultation, rather than providing products. Payments are an important part of these interactions, but they extend much further to include permissions, information sharing, applications and registrations, complaints and resolution as well as digital services (like e-health). Examples include submitting tax returns, applying for a passport or licence and claiming medicare and welfare benefits. At the Federal government level, the bulk of transactions are driven through the Department of Human Services (DHS, including Medicare and Centrelink), the Australian Taxation Office (ATO) and the Department of Immigration.

The Commonwealth Department of Human Services (DHS) is amongst the most complex of these government 'beasts' dealing with most Australians across health and welfare programmes. According to DHS, last financial year it paid out $165 billion, took 57 million phone calls and looked into 108,000 fraud line tip-offs. 25. 4 million people walked into its shopfronts, there were 115 million visits to its website, while 124 million transactions went through online accounts and 61 million through mobile apps.[18]

Broadly defined, a transaction begins with information gathering, search and inquiry, and is followed by ongoing support. Different channels are often used for different parts of a transaction or different aspects of a customer relationship. Complex issue resolution is typically done via calls or face to face, whereas a simple check of a tax account balance is easily done online. The trick for governments and private businesses is to move customers online for the least complex activities, and then migrate them across for the full transaction and relationship life cycle.

Deloitte Access Economics has estimated that across Australian state and federal governments there are 811 million transactions each year,[19] approximately 40% of which are still completed using the traditional channels of telephone, post and face-to-face.[20]

Arguably, Deloitte underestimates the number of government interactions that take place in practice. For instance, voting is an interaction that is not typically considered as lending itself to go online any time soon. However, there is absolutely no reason why online voting can't become a reality in the future (see Fiqure 4). Indeed, many countries are leading the way in online voting.[21] Over 30% of Estonians participating in the vote gave their vote over the internet.[22] Closer to home the last NSW election piloted online voting.[23]

Like voting, education might be considered a transaction that can't go online. However, the rapid growth of MOOCs (massive open online courses) is pushing tertiary education online. Similarly, censuses, infrastructure management and even national security all offer enormous potential for digitisation.

The biggest prize: Better targeting of government services

Most discussions of benefits from digitisation start and finish with customer service improvements and direct efficiencies in reduced customer service costs. Often forgotten are the bigger opportunities for compliance, risk management, payment integrity, and programme targetting with savings far beyond direct efficiencies. Integrity and compliance in government payments offers one of the greatest opportunities for efficiency and effectiveness of government spending. Even a small improvement in payments for health and welfare would yield benefits worth many billions each year.

For example, in primary health care savings of 5% or more have been achieved by private health insurance through 'big data' initiatives. These initiatives focus on identifying payments which are the result of errors, abuse, or fraud.[24] The DNP initiative in the United States[25] is delivering similar benefits in welfare compliance. DNP allows agencies to check various data sources for payment eligibility, at the time of payment and any time in the payment lifecycle.

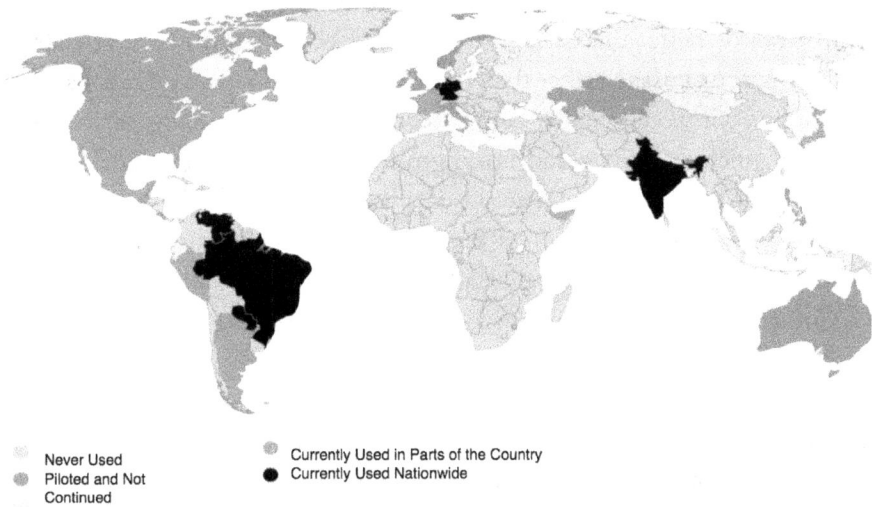

Never Used
Piloted and Not
Continued

Currently Used in Parts of the Country
Currently Used Nationwide

Figure 4: E-voting around the world

Identifying savings or revenue opportunities from better government practices or better targeted spending requires access to quality data. Through digitisation, governments can increase easy access to large databases for analysis. Identifying errors, abuse or defrauding of big dollar government programmes, especially health and welfare, has been a source of significant government savings around the world, but real time access to quality data sets is a prerequisite to realising these opportunities.

Once these datasets are well established and accessible, they will also provide a much better fact base for better targeting of government programmes and spending, beyond just compliance. The real impact of government programmes on key outcomes like employment or health is rarely measured well. In practice, it is inevitable that much of that money could be better spent. But until we can get access to integrated data sets on individuals' health, welfare, education and access to programmes, as well as the impact of these programmes over time, refocusing spending will continue to be extremely difficult, powered by emotional political resistance.

Similarly, access to quality data for traffic movements would allow a shift towards better infrastructure funding models, with road user charges reflecting actual usage rather than using fuel usage as a proxy. Perhaps more importantly, it would enable better targeting of road funding payments to 'owners' (including State and Local governments) based on actual usage.[26] This is only possible if the relevant data is captured and used.

Likewise, quality data offers the potential for better use of assets like roads and carparks. Whether through improved signalling or real time access to information about congestion, improved infrastructure utilisation is typically much cheaper than new investment.

The skills and system changes required to deliver these savings shouldn't be underestimated. Quality 'big data' analysts are a rare breed, combining sharp commercial acumen, with extremely strong quantitative skills alongside strong systems and database capabilities. They also require strong leadership and organisational skills, because so much of what is required demands working across many agencies and departments. Most importantly, these people and teams require support from the top, as we shall see in Chapter 6.

The direct benefits to governments and taxpayers

The direct benefits to governments and citizens of digitising government are also much larger and broader in scope than is typically realised, totally over $27 billion according to Deloitte Access.

There are the obvious direct cost savings, but the benefits extend to earlier payment and significant reductions in storage and advertising spend.

Direct cost savings: Traditional non-digital channels are expensive for governments. According to Deloitte Access, each face to face transaction is conservatively estimated at $16.90, with postal transactions costing $12.79, and telephone calls costing $6.60. In contrast, digital transactions cost 40 cents, and this is likely to fall over time as technology improves and scale advantages are harnessed. The UK government has found similar savings in its Digital Efficiency report.[27]

Of the total transactions in Federal government, the biggest contributors are DHS, ATO and Department of Immigration. At the state level it is

Roads and Maritime Services, Fair Trading and Births, Deaths and Marriages registry. Of the total 811 million current transactions with government, 320 million transactions are still offline.

Deloitte estimates that the benefits to government will reach $1.7 billion per year in savings just by halving the current non-digital transactions or $17.5 billion in present value terms.[28] These savings come at least partly from the very significant labour costs in traditional roles including keyboard operators, call centre workers and enquiry clerks.

No doubt, criticism of an aggressive digitisation strategy will focus on the loss of some of these jobs. In reality, many or most of these workers can be trained to move into higher value added roles, such as a focus on compliance (e.g. the identification of fraud, abuse or errors in government payments) or providing digital education to customers and citizens (see chapter 6). Regardless, rising productivity does not increase unemployment other than in the very short term and, most importantly, it is the ultimate source of rising incomes.[29]

Digital payments are typically also made earlier, because of the opportunity costs for citizens of traditional payments (e.g. travelling to a storefront or sending through the mail). Deloitte has estimated this to be as high as $543 million per year, or a lifetime benefit of $5.6 billion.

Reduced storage costs and advertising spend: Most paper based government transactions need to be stored and yet digital storage is significantly cheaper than paper storage. The National Archive is currently reviewing its storage strategy, and recently estimated that paper storage costs exceed $150 million per year across government departments.[30] A strategy to shift to digital storage of all paper documentation offers significant savings over time.

One of the more interesting by-products of digitising government is that it provides the opportunity to personalise communication at a very low cost. Highly targeted messaging is extremely valuable – Facebook and Google are able to generate extraordinary advertising income because their ads are highly personalised and targeted, to the point that they aren't typically perceived to be intrusive. Governments have a wealth of information about citizens – where they live, what they do for work, how much they earn and where they school their kids, amongst other things. In communication terms, this is gold.

The Federal government's advertising spend per year exceeds $100 million, and postage costs of direct mail advertising exceed $250 million.[31] Moving users online offers the potential for highly targeted online advertising with a corresponding reduction in government advertising spend. It also offers opportunities to 'cross-sell' new digital services to an engaged audience. With vastly reduced advertising costs we can reasonably assume governments will increase their volume and quality of communication with citizens.

Improved customer experience and customer savings: Again and again, we see that customers across private and public sectors have a strong preference for using internet or telephone over other channels.[32] When there is choice between using the mobile or internet channels versus some other channel for contacting government, the internet is preferred.

This is primarily because of convenience, particularly the time and cost savings involved. In addition, mobile and internet channels are available 24/7 in a world where we are used to accessing services when we want them.

However there is mounting evidence that digital preference goes deeper than this, and goes to the enormous frustration of traditional channels. Ironically, the experience of the banks is that moving customers online and keeping them online improves customer satisfaction. At the very least, we know that digital channels can achieve similar satisfaction levels to face to face channels.

Successful digital transactions – those that keep people online and resolve the issue immediately – offer enormous potential for improved customer service. We know one of the greatest frustrations with all government interactions is the time it takes to receive a response to the issue, as against the outcome itself.[33] Linked to this is extreme frustration in waiting an extended period of time to be served, or dealing with someone in person or on the phone who doesn't seem to understand the issue.

In addition, most of us have spent time travelling to and from a government office in order to complete a basic transaction, like registering a car or applying for a passport. Of course, the travel is just the beginning, because the wait time that follows can be even more frustrating. In addition, non-digital channels require additional spend on transport and postage costs.

Deloitte conservatively estimate[34] these savings at $846 million once around half of current offline transactions are taken online, with a lifetime value of around $8.6 billion.

3

TRANSFORMING PUBLIC SERVICE DELIVERY

- Broad-reaching digitisation of government can drive reforms that traditional political processes can't
- Crowdsourcing citizen and customer content will drive unprecedented accountability for service delivery
- Opening up government data to third party developers will deliver rapid innovation in applications for citizens to engage with government
- Digitisation will result in innovative new services at previously unachievable costs (e.g. higher education)
- The full potential of digital government will only be realised in combination with genuine contestability of public services

Like most urban or regional councils, the city of Boston struggles with road maintenance. Harsh, snowy winters with salted roads worsen the problem, with crews patching 19,000 potholes each year. Inspecting these roads regularly is a huge expense, and is not particularly accurate anyway.

Many local governments around the world have experimented with citizen reporting of road conditions. All suffer from lack of participation. It's just too much of a hassle to fill out forms, remember the exact spot and deliver the details to the right place.

In 2012, that changed for Boston. Officials began testing an app that detected bumps in the road, using the accelerometer - a motion detector - on citizens' phones. GPS recorded the location, and the phone transmitted it to a remote server hosted by Amazon's Web services division. Once a bump is detected and fixed, the users who report the bump get credit for their contribution.

The initial prototype was developed for $45,000 by a private developer, but there were problems. The application picked up speed humps, manholes and other disturbances. So the challenge was thrown out to a network of experts offering them a modest prize, $25,000. Three groups contributed to the solution – a set of algorithms to distinguish between different types of bumps – and shared the prize money. For a total of $70,000, Boston had developed a solution for a seemingly intractable problem.

According to the Boston official looking after the project, Nigel Jacob, "This technology ... essentially creates a new way for people to donate their data in solving public-good challenges".[35]

Closer to home, local councils are experimenting with less sophisticated apps, but across a broader range of areas. 'Snap Send Solve' was developed as part of a Victorian Government 'App My State' competition in 2010. The result is a mobile app that takes all the thinking out of reporting to local authorities. Whether a pothole, a broken swing or graffiti, it allows citizens to report simply and easily to local authorities, including every council in Australia as well as water, gas and electricity companies.

The app uses GPS to establish your location, it identifies who manages incidents within that particular area and then sends through relevant information and any related image to the correct contact. Whilst it lacks the sophistication of the 'Boston Bump', with sixty thousand users and some good early results it is a big step in the direction of digitising customer feedback to road owners in Australia.

The essence of the traditional model of government is centrally driven service delivery with one-way broadcast of the features and benefits. The service is developed by government, it tells citizens what government is offering, and that's the end of it. Feedback is rarely possible, and definitely not encouraged.

Citizens and customers in modern market driven democracies see this, quite rightly, as totally out of touch with the rest of our lives. If we don't like what a private sector vendor is selling us, we can choose to go elsewhere, give them feedback, or both. Good business people listen to the feedback and adapt. That cycle of feedback and adaptation has driven years of innovation, productivity gains and entrepreneurship. People have come to believe that government cannot and will not work this way. Bureaucrats accustomed to managing uncontested monopolies and public sector unions conspire to make the situation worse.

This is where Government 2.0 comes in. At its best, Government 2.0 is made up of five big ideas: Crowdsourced content, competitive application development, open access to government data, contested public services and digital service innovation. On their own, these ideas are not new. What is new is the way online platforms can make them easier, and can combine them into very powerful means of delivering better government. It's only where all or most of these components are in place that we are likely to get the best results. The central thesis of this chapter is that broad digital transformation of government offers enormous potential and that journey is just beginning. Most importantly, we need to accelerate it.

Putting the backpack on the monkey's back: Crowdsourcing content and contributions

As a young management consultant I worked with a seasoned manager who had a wonderful saying when things got tough and our client team was unreasonably demanding. He would talk about 'putting the backpack on the monkey's back', meaning that we needed to put the client team to work to help solve the problem. This had two great benefits. First, more work was done. Second, the client team stopped sitting back and complaining about what we were doing, and started to solve problems for themselves. I was always amazed at how well it worked, but in hindsight I shouldn't have been. There is a great wisdom in harnessing crowds, and engagement is the first step in finding solutions to hard problems.

'Crowdsourced content and contribution' means citizens can provide direct and well-structured feedback to a public service provider. If a service provider has heard the same complaint one thousand times, it's hard to remain unresponsive. Once enough cars have driven over a new pot hole and reported it to council, only the most arrogant council would sit on its hands.

Of course, crowdsourcing content is not a new idea, even if capturing it by clever means online is new. Neighbourhood Watch has been around in the US and Australia as far back as the 1960s in the United States, with more recent establishment in various Australian states. The guiding principle is that, in many cases the community is better suited to detecting and reporting potential crimes than police. By educating community members on how to do this, and providing a channel to do so, the police harness voluntary resources to improve crime prevention across all communities.

The advent of the internet and smart phones has just made this much cheaper, easier and more attractive. Rating teachers, hospitals, roads and doctors can be done much faster and with little cost to the content provider. There is always a question about the quality of the content and the potential for 'rigged rating' but companies like Ebay, Uber and Amazon have demonstrated that this can be overcome. Indeed one of the most remarkable examples of crowdsourcing is the movie rating website 'Rotten Tomatoes' which has such a deep user base and reliable rating that it can quickly swing the success or failure of a new movie release.

Naming and shaming institutions, and individual professions, is always controversial, but we do it now. We do it in making decisions about where we send our kids to school or university, or which doctor to see. The idea of taking it online is simply a means of amplifying and accelerating a process that already happens in the real world.

Ratemyteachers.com does exactly that – it asks students to rate school and university educators on their performance. Similar sites are springing up around the world for rating schools, doctors and hospitals.[36] The launch of *Iwantgreatcare. co.uk* in the UK in 2008 caused a storm of controversy. It was launched by a UK doctor with a focus on rating hospitals, medical centres, doctors and other health services. Professionals disliked the scrutiny, but the rating system has proliferated with some hospitals now receiving over 100,000 reviews.

While many of these applications have been developed without any government data or sponsorship, some of the most powerful solutions do have government support. The UK National Health Service is leading the world in this area, with NHS Choices. This website doesn't just provide details about health services available across the UK, it also provides detailed survey results on each service, and allows users to rate the services themselves and to see other people's ratings. The combination of objective fact based data, survey outputs and customer ratings is a powerful public sector example of a reputational tool first developed by Ebay and more recently Uber.

NHS Choices does not hold back in providing extremely frank feedback on the performance of hospitals, doctors and health practitioners where the crowdsourced data justifies it. In a system where customers have a high degree of choice, this kind of system is very powerful in empowering consumers to shift to better providers, and driving the lower performers to improve.

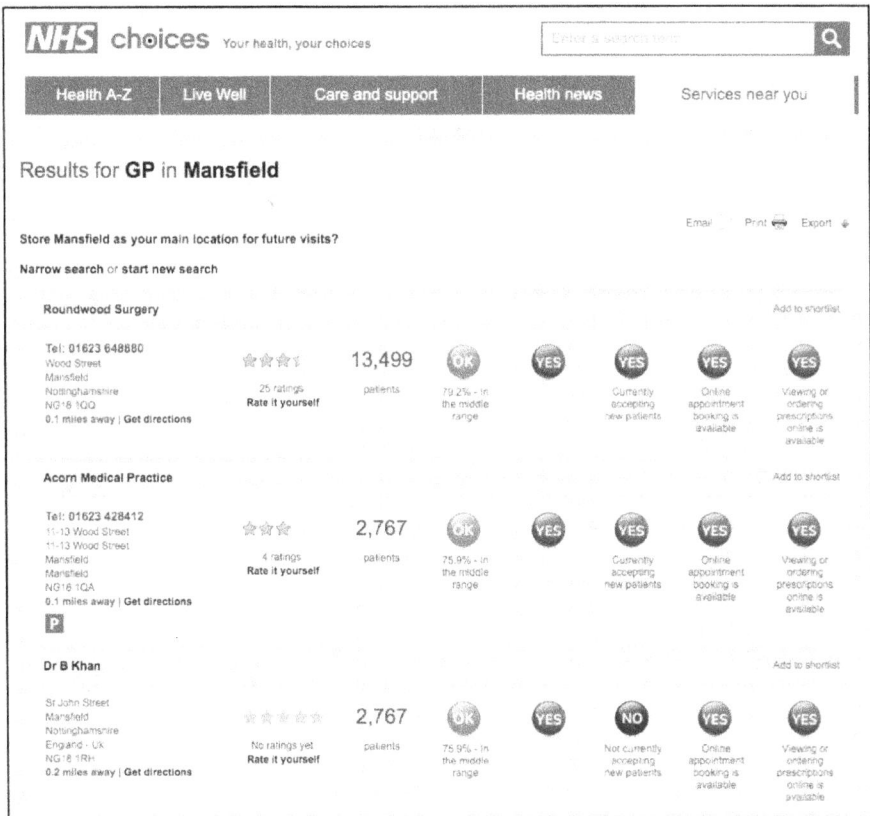

Figure 5: NHS Choices: Hospital and Medical Centre Ratings

Letting a thousand flowers bloom: Competitive application development

When the first internet boom was at its peak in the late 1990s, it was widely believed that first mover advantage was the key to cashing in on a good idea. Like many faddish ideas, this was proven to be wrong. Yahoo beat Google to search by several years, but Google won with a clean simple user interface and genius in its search algorithm. Myspace beat Facebook to social media, but Facebook eventually won. The truth is that competition between multiple providers typically leads to rapid innovation, and seemingly small innovations can make a large difference to take-up and ultimate success.

'Competitive application development' means governments open up public data, subject to personal confidentiality constraints, to allow third parties to develop applications. This offers enormous potential for innovation around the user interface, the use of the data and the potential to draw in additional feedback. We know that many of the greatest digital breakthroughs in recent years – Google's search, Facebook's social networks – came about as result of ferocious competition between many developers to solve a real world problem.

Throughout the world, we are seeing the potential of smart, typically young, developers solving real problems for government. One of the most successful programmes is *Code for America*, which is now extending its reach to *Code for Australia*. *Code for America* (and Australia) provides year long fellowships for 'rockstar geeks' to get involved with solving the problems of government, from the outside.

The problems solved range from cleaning up streets in Seattle through to selecting schools in Boston in the face of extraordinarily complex rules about eligibility. In each case, coders used datasets made available to develop simple applications. Using traditional development approaches, this would have taken two years and would have cost two million dollars, according to Jennifer Pahlka, the CEO of *Code for America*.

Hackathons are a powerful way to kickstart a focus on particular areas of focus. The Federal government as well as many state governments have been going down this path, along with many other countries around the world (e.g. Singapore). Whilst the results are sometimes encouraging, there is often a lack of guidance about the government's priorities and strategic focus. These competitions are much more likely to yield high impact results with a sharper focus on areas of policy and delivery that are a strategic priority. That way, governments have a strong incentive to follow up with additional funding and guidance where necessary.

Setting information free: Open access to government data

One of the great projects of governments in the 21st century is providing better access to government information. In some cases this will be highly restricted private information, like health records or education records, enabling individuals to permit access to businesses and their service providers to make better decisions. However, better decisions by government depend on accessing aggregated information to compare the outcomes of different approaches or just different organisations in the provision of government services.

Applications developed by governments or (as is more likely) third parties will need to be able to access individual data (with appropriate permissions) or aggregated data to evaluate and compare services. One of the best known examples of this in Australia in recent years is the MySchool website, which opens up data on school performance and financials. It is widely used by parents to compare schools, and is increasing accountability and transparency across both public and private schools. As we will see below, however, the full impact of this important initiative will always be limited by lack of contestability (e.g. freedom in choice of schools). Similar initiatives are popping up around the world in many different public services. For instance, in the UK the Quality Care Commission has a very simple website rating all health and social care organisations.[37]

Central to this is providing open access to strategic data sets through application programming interfaces (APIs). Australia has been going down this path in recent years, as Pia Waugh, the Director of Gov 2.0 in the Department of Finance tells us:

> We've gone from 500 data sets to 7000 data sets in two years. We
> have agencies now knocking down the door wanting to publish open
> data. So we've had a huge amount of success not just publishing

data, but also chaining [sic] the culture of agencies.[38]

But as she is quick to point out, the Federal Governments' data.gov.
au initiative needs more focus and support from across departments and
agencies. Anyone can retail the services of government, but they need to get
access to the government data through an API.

Most of us accept that releasing data on public services will help to
improve them, but this is difficult to achieve in practice and requires strong
pressure from the top. Good progress is occurring in pockets, for instance
Geoscience Australia and the ABS are licencing much of their output using
creative commons licences which permit others to freely use and remix it.
However, more focus and urgency is now critical.

Contestability and choice in the provision of public services

Perhaps the most striking difference between many public services, and
private service provision, is lack of competition, choice or contestability.
Markets typically abhor monopolies – given time they wear them down,
even if regulators don't, and the disruption is often driven by technology.

Contestability is often much more difficult in the provision of public
services, because of legislated government monopolies. Public instincts
are (quite rightly) that governments can do better. To the frustration of
the general public, governments have been relatively slow to unleash the
benefits of contestable service provision. Much of this is due to resistance,
often vigorous, particularly from public sector unions.

The reality is that digital transformation of public services will always
be limited without some element of choice or contestability.[39] Applications
comparing performance of schools, doctors and hospitals are all well and
good. However, if consumers of those services have no genuine choice, and
leaders in these organisations have limited discretion to respond by changing
their organisations, then the impact will be limited.

On the other hand, choice or contestability combined with digital
transformation offers enormous potential. This can come in two forms.

The first is when consumers have genuine choice. If parents have detailed data and crowdsourced feedback on school performance, and they have significant choice about where they send their children then digital government initiatives will have far greater impact. We already have significant elements of choice in Australia between schools, hospitals, GPs, employment service providers, childcare centres and universities.

The second is when managers have autonomy to make changes to respond to benchmarks versus other providers. In a school setting this means principals have a high degree of autonomy in selection of teachers, in setting the curriculum and in testing and adopting new education techniques.

For instance, in 2012 a comparison of the performance of Sydney Water with Victorian water utilities showed that the Victorians were delivering comparable service levels at a lower cost. Based on these benchmarks, Sydney water drove a highly effective reform strategy based on 'beating the market'. Service levels rose, productivity improved by almost 20% and staff engagement and industrial relations have improved markedly.[40]

In regional areas, choice between service providers is more difficult, but contestability is still possible through benchmarking of comparable service providers. For instance, in Australia, the National Health Performance Agency publishes online performance over time on critical indicators, like emergency department waiting times (Figure 6). Whether or not patients have genuine choice across hospitals, this sort of online reporting, combined with managerial discretion within hospitals, is likely to drive performance over time.

Government services are well suited to benchmarking and choice, because often they involve lots of small units of performance (e.g. schools, hospitals or job service providers). As a matter of priority, governments need to allow third parties access to this data, encouraging consumers to make better informed choices. All of this is made irrelevant if governments take away choice from consumers.

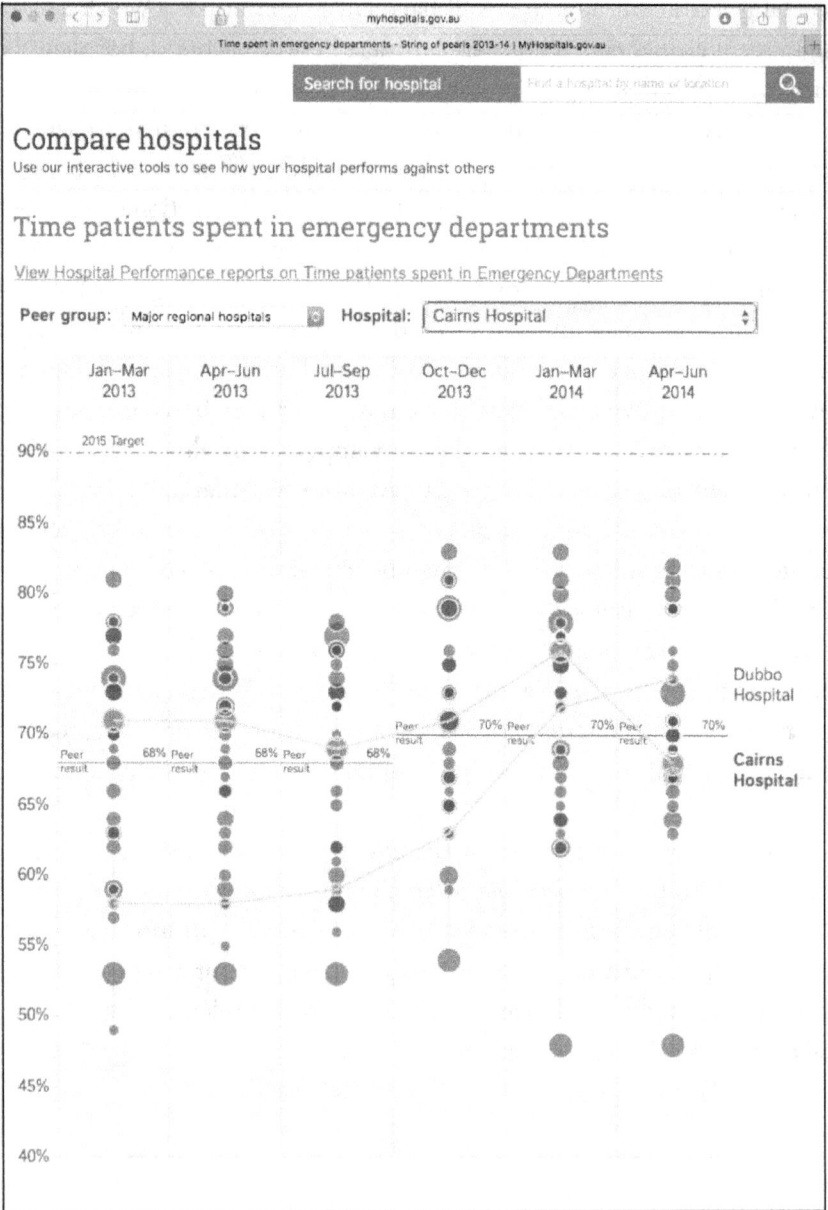

Figure 6: Patients seen by ED within 4 hours – major regional hospitals

Innovative digital service delivery and support

In many cases government services themselves can now be delivered through use of 'digital channels'. This goes well beyond just capturing and managing data in digital form – it means provision of a digital service, traditionally provided face to face. Obviously, this can offer cost savings to government and citizens, but it can also mean providing services in much more innovative ways than traditional channels.

For example, an increasing portion of tertiary education can be provided digitally. Indeed, the productivity gains in higher education are beyond what we might expect in most sectors. A superstar lecturer can now be accessed by students at every university in the world.[41] While there have been false starts in the use of technology for higher education, it is now having a very real impact. Most university lecturers now provide the lectures online, and increasingly whole courses are provided online for example through 'MOOCs' (massive open online courses). In 2004 Salmond Khan put his university tutorials and lectures onto YouTube. This soon turned into the Khan Academy serving millions of students from all backgrounds across the world.

In health, there is little doubt that the coming years will see far greater focus on patient focused care which manages all aspects of persons health, with a particular focus on keeping them healthy and out of hospital. Nowhere is that more important than where there is serious chronic disease like diabetes, cardiovascular disease and respiratory disease. But the idea that this is best achieved through a regular consultation makes no sense. On some days, a phone conversation is the best option. At other times, the doctor will simply want access to personal data online. Sometimes a video-conference is the right solution.

Sensors now offer the opportunity to manage a person's health in real time, with practitioners getting direct access to data to identify problems and quickly address them.[42] Telehealth is also gaining momentum, particularly for well suited services (e.g. psychiatry) and in more isolated regions. All of this will require significant change to the medical benefits system, but change that is more than overdue. Part of the opportunity here is to rethink the role traditional GP consultations as the centrepiece of our primary healthcare system. Appropriate sharing of information can make much better (and cheaper) use of allied health professionals, like pharmacists and practice nurses.

Similar use of digital services is emerging in other unexpected areas of government. Technology is increasingly useful in crime prevention, via use of CCTV cameras and DNA testing. Indeed there is increasing evidence that technology has had a very significant impact on crime rates, even if new types of crime are emerging through use of technology. In national security and border protection, we are rapidly replacing manned combatants with unmanned digital driven vehicles.

Bringing all of Government 2.0 together to transform public services

It is difficult to find examples where governments have combined all of these elements of Government 2.0 to transform their service provision. Even the Boston Bump example introducing this chapter doesn't have any real contestability between road maintenance providers, nor does it provide any real digital service, beyond feedback to the person reporting the bump. At a pinch, it would be possible to benchmark one region against another. Nonetheless, there is no limit on providing drivers with digital guidance on the quality of a road, based on crowdsourced information.

A number of public services lend themselves beautifully to deploying all aspects of Government 2.0. Pre-school, primary school, secondary school and tertiary all offer great potential for an integrated set of initiatives. Services can be competitive and benchmarked, performance evaluation can be crowdsourced, aggregate test data can be opened up to third party application developers and some services can be provided digitally.[43]

Health, too, offers great potential, across hospital care, primary care or allied health. In each case, consumers have options, feedback can be obtained easily, and there is no shortage of data from which to develop very powerful applications. The key to all of this is enlisting customers and citizens to apply pressure on service providers to deliver better value.

As we have seen, Australian governments have started on the journey towards Government 2.0. However, we don't yet have an education system where all schools, universities and training organisations are rated and compete based on those outcomes. The same can be said of health, job services, aged care and childcare. Government data is being released at an accelerating pace, but not necessarily the data that will reshape policy and service delivery quickly. Hackathons are widely used by many governments, but they are not focused on the policy challenges digital transformation could address.

We need a much more strategic integrated approach across governments. For instance, *Code for America* focuses on four strategic priorities – health, economic development, safety and justice and communication and engagement. It is focused on key problems in each area, deploying its people and teams strategically to solve real problems.

Top order policy problems need to be agreed upon, and the powerful Government 2.0 toolkit can be unleashed to solve these problems.

4

MOBILISING THE SILENT MAJORITY: REINVENTING CITIZENSHIP AND REGULATION

- Digital engagement is shaping a new model of citizenship better suited for modern, time-poor citizens
- Engaging citizens to campaign against wasteful spending is a particularly clear example of this
- Traditional government regulation can make way for customer and citizen driven regulation without the involvement of government
- Governments should encourage this new model of citizenship and regulation to drive badly needed reforms
- Increasing trust between government and citizens is a crucial first step in this journey

My first political memories are of the 1975 Federal election, when I had just turned ten. I was at primary school in a tiny town in southern NSW when the Governor-General intervened to force a double dissolution election. Everyone seemed to have a view about this, and many were active in supporting their view.

At my primary school, we had endless debates and even mimicked an election campaign with parties formed, campaign speeches given (which were recorded on video – almost unheard of at the time) and we all voted. A large part of the local population got involved with the election campaigns, on all sides (it was a contest between the Liberal Party, National Party and Labor), and I stood with my father at the booth on polling day. Opposite us was one of Dad's employees, who was a staunch Labor man. I still have vivid memories of the clash between "Turn on the Lights" with "Shame Fraser Shame". That night, we went to a very well attended post-election party to see the results emerging from the Canberra Tally room on black and white TV.

What I saw was a level of participation in politics and civic issues that has been in decline ever since. Party memberships have fallen, attendance in campaign or protest events is not like the days of the 60s or 70s, and many of those who do get involved have a direct interest in doing so, such as being members of a union.

This trend away from electoral participation is most pronounced amongst the young, and this appears to be more than just a life-cycle effect.[44] Despite this, there is evidence of rising levels of volunteering, albeit for activities like sport and recreation, particularly by parents supporting their children's activities.[45]

A new type of citizenship?

Lurking beneath the volunteering data is an unexpected trend: The rise of a new type of political and civic participation. This includes online petitions, online polls and politically oriented social media. Often dismissed as 'slacktivism' – a modern form of activism when you can't be bothered to march the streets – the development is important, because it tells us people still want to participate in civic society, even if they don't want to participate in traditional ways.

Many citizens are time poor like never before. Many families have two parents who work outside the home to pay for their cost of living, particularly housing, just as commuting times have increased in our cities. There is a deep natural instinct for humans to participate in their community, but we need means of doing so that recognise the 'impatience' of the modern citizen.

Of course, online 'slactivism' is not genuine citizenship, because mostly it identifies problems rather than delivering solutions. The challenge is how to get people to use their 'hands, not just their voices' as Jennifer Pahlka, CEO of *Code for America*, puts it. That is, how do we mobilise people to do things rather than just scream about government failure?

Code for America has focused much of its efforts on developing digital tools to enhance citizenship – what we might call 'civic apps'. One example comes from Boston, where in the height of a snowy winter fire hydrants were getting buried, and local residents were digging out their footpaths, but ignoring adjacent hydrants. So a clever developer developed 'adopt-a-hydrant' whereby local residents could commit to digging out a hydrant near where they live, winning points for doing so.[46] By using game dynamics, such as being able to name your hydrant and the ability for users to 'steal' ownership if it is not done in a timely manner, the app went viral.

The basic idea caught on, and soon after Honolulu developed a similar app for keeping batteries charged in tsunami sirens.[47] Seattle developed an app for citizens to adopt storm water drains. Nine cities have now developed similar apps.

According to Jennifer Pahlka, government needs to work more like the internet itself – open, regenerative – government as a platform for people to help themselves and help others.

Citizens as spending vigilantes

One area where this offers great potential is in preventing government waste. With fast growth in expenditure, particularly in areas like health and aged care, government budgets have rarely looked so bad. Not surprisingly, any sign of government misspending is treated with outrage by the electorate. We often hear of perceived misuse of government 'entitlements'[48] or wasted money in government tenders.[49]

The public's focus is heavily skewed to wastage we already see online. For example, politicians' entitlements and government tender details are currently easily accessed. Indeed, the entitlements information is not available real time or in particularly digestible form, but at least it is available. In total, this expenditure is only a tiny fraction of total government spending, but it attracts disproportionate attention. Similarly, when cost benchmarks were released on school building projects under the previous Labor government, citizens and journalists were quick to make government accountable for its spending.

There is real potential to extend this to other areas of government expenditure. Why shouldn't patients be able to see how health service providers spend taxpayers' money, benchmarked against their comparable peers? Why shouldn't citizens be able to compare the cost of building a new road, or upgrading an old one, against reasonable benchmarks? Why shouldn't citizens see how much it costs to build a new school hall, compared with other states or regions?

Private sector organisations are using this technique to drive down costs. For instance, BUPA (a private health insurer) is publishing price information on surgical procedures such as hip replacements. Their objective is to put downward price pressure on surgeons, who are, in some cases, charging "exorbitant" fees.[50] This is part of a broader push by health insurers to cut waste in the health system and get a better deal for consumers. As the largest insurer in the market, the government can and should do the same.

As politicians struggle to deal with the powerful vested interests of unions, businesses and activist lobby groups, transparency of government spending has the potential to be a cleansing force. In the past this was hardly achievable, but almost every aspect of government expenditure can now be accessed, and benchmarked either within Australia, or with other countries. This kind of information has transformed practices in the private sector, as underperforming businesses and people are faced with facts that are beyond realistic dispute. We need the same kind of transparency in government.

Citizens as regulators

Uber, the ride sharing application, has caught the world off-guard. Based on a very sharp customer focus and an attractive model for drivers, growth has been stratospheric. Users get to book their cars on their phones, see the location of the car from the moment it is booked, learn the name and customer rating of the driver and payment is automatic. Poorly rated drivers are spurned, and peak needs are met with fee premiums that are usually reasonable.

The model works for one simple reason – the government regulated traditional taxi system is less attractive to customers and drivers than the customer regulated Uber. There are few purer examples of a customer regulated market outgunning a highly regulated government alternative.

So if a large number of customers and drivers prefer Uber, what were governments doing wrong, or are the customers and drivers just cheating the system? It is true that there have been tax issues, although in most jurisdictions these are being sorted out with little impact on the success of the model. The fundamental point is that when power is shifted to the customer – through up to date easy to digest information and customer based rating – the government can step back and allow customers to do their own regulation. AirBnB is a similar sobering illustration of how an over-regulated industry leaves everyone worse off.

Central to the success of these apps is the rating and reputation model first popularised by EBay in the late 1990s. Creating a market typically requires some element of trust between buyer and seller, and nothing builds trust more than reputation. Ebay realised they could create online reputations, based on customer rating systems. The idea took hold immediately, and created one of the world's first and most enduring online marketplaces.

The growth of government regulation is one of the most frustrating and costly business trends for business people throughout the developed world. Few politicians in this modern era have meaningful business experience, and the political bias to more regulation is strong. In the parliament, you could be forgiven for thinking that productivity is measured by the number of new bills that are passed, rather than by delivering better outcomes for citizens.

The potential to replace heavy handed government regulation with lighter touch digitally driven customer regulation is only just beginning. In the world of finance, crowd-funding and new means of financing businesses and households are flourishing, without needing heavy handed government intervention. In vocational education, digital rating of service providers could address many of the recent challenges faced in that sector.

Even a subject as fraught and basic as how to get country of origin food labelling right could be solved using digital technologies. As food safety and the 'story' behind products becomes more important to consumers, the country of origin of the food has become a political hot button. What seems like a simple problem turns out to be quite complex, with the need to differentiate the source of ingredients, processing and packaging. On top of this, the source can change several times over the course of a season, particularly for fresh food.

Already, it is possible to download apps to scan barcodes and get nutrition information, websites, vendors and prices.[51] This could easily be extended to include country of origin labelling, allowing far more detailed information, with regular updating, than is possible with physical labelling. Once the standards and systems are settled, applications will develop quickly. In-store scanners could be used for those without smart phones. It is then up to citizens to decide how they want to use this information, or whether they want to access it in the first place.

Central to this is a need to build trust between the application and user. To the extent that government is directly involved, that level of trust will need to build over time, as it has with Ebay, Uber and other reputation based markets.

We are only just beginning to see how technology can redefine citizenship, and how we can pass over regulation to citizens and customers. By handing power to citizens and consumers, we can take pressure off a creaking political system that overregulates as a response to the shrill voice of a narrowly focused vested interest. Citizens and consumers can drive the reforms that the political process struggles to deliver.

5

SUPPORTING A DIGITAL ECONOMY

- Digital government extends to facilitating the rapid growth of the digital economy
- The most important role of government is to eliminate regulation that impedes digital disruption, and avoid new regulation that inhibits disrupters
- Other roles of government in the digital economy include:
    - Facilitating the growth of digital infrastructure
    - Supporting skill development and the commercialisation of government funded research
    - Encouraging innovative suppliers and service providers through government purchasing processes
    - Supporting the development of common standards

According to Amara's Law, we overestimate the impact of a new technology in the short run and underestimate the impact in the long run.[52] Many of the ideas in the 'dot com' era of the late 1990s were ahead of their time. Fifteen years on, most of those ideas are now a reality, in one form or another. Given the rapid pace of digital disruption across the economy in industries ranging from taxis, to health to agriculture and financial services, when it comes to digitisation Amara's long run is arriving in many parts of our economy. In practice, that means that the impacts and benefits of digital disruption are now likely to come thick and fast.

The benefits of a digital economy are increasingly clear. The McKinsey Global Institute has calculated around a fifth of GDP growth in advanced economies over the past five years has arisen from the Internet and associated technologies. 75 per cent of this growth is occurring in sectors not traditionally seen as 'technology' industries.[53] The real benefits of the digital economy don't come through job and wealth creation in start-ups, but through the take-up of digital applications out in traditional industries, like farming, mining, retail, and banking. Deloitte estimates the digital economy to be over 5% of GDP,[54] and one-third of the Australian economy faces imminent and major disruption.[55]

Many have argued that this disruption will destroy jobs permanently. Studies of potential jobs losses often come up with big numbers, although few focus enough attention on the new jobs that are created.[56] The loss of sailing ships, horse and carts and bullock drays didn't lead to permanent unemployment, and much technology increases the productivity of labour, not just replacing it.[57]

Until recently, Australia's 'digital readiness' has been stalling relative to peers. In 2014, the Tuft University Digital Evolution Index rated Australia as a 'stall out' country.[58] In other words, we had achieved a high rate of digital evolution in the past, but now risk falling behind. According to the World Economic Forum Global technology index, Australia's ranking fell from 9th to 18th over the eight years until 2013, before a small recovery to 16th in 2015. Similarly, the International Telecommunications Union ICT development index showed deterioration from 15th to 21st in the five years until 2012, before recovering to 13th in 2015.

Uniquely among OECD members, the share of Australians using the internet for their most recent interaction with government fell during the latter years of the last government.[59] This was accompanied by a fall in satisfaction levels for online interactions with the Commonwealth government between 2007 and 2011.

Network performance is only a small part of the problem. An obsession with high speed fibre to the home was almost certainly one of the reasons for poor overall performance during recent years. The political and regulatory environment, the context for business innovation, technology skills of the population and usage levels are all relevant factors driving digital readiness.

The difficult question is what role can the government play to accelerate the benefits of a digital economy? This is a critical question for liberals or conservatives, because their natural bias is to say that governments should leave this to the private sector.

It is clear that governments have been slow to embrace digital disruption for their own services, and need to get their house in order before lecturing the private sector on what it should do. But governments can play a crucial role in knocking down barriers to empower entrepreneurs. They can provide infrastructure, set standards (where necessary) and support fundamental R & D and skill development.

Perhaps most importantly, governments can also eliminate redundant regulation impeding the growth of the digital economy. Eliminating red tape is crucially important and feasible, as digitisation switches power from producers to consumers. We have seen that much of the traditionally regulatory role of government can be done better by consumers. Governments can also unleash an entrepreneurial focus on government services and regulation, but they have to be prepared to abolish legislation that protects strong vested interest.

Deregulating the digital economy

The digital economy is disruptive, almost by definition. One of the biggest barriers to digitisation of the economy is government regulation, holding back innovation and creating unnecessary costs for innovators. These barriers can crop up in unexpected places, and are usually driven by vested interest.

For example, 'sharing economy' applications for ridesharing (Uber) or accommodation (AirBnB) are disrupting traditional old slow-moving industries. Government regulation is threatening to impede these innovations. These two examples are just the beginning with fast growing 'sharing economy' applications emerging in car sharing (Getaround), contract work (Task rabbit), parking (Parkhound), small loans (Lending club) and even pet minding (Dogvacay). Beyond this, in books, music, media, photography, finance and elsewhere, digital disruption is broad reaching.

It is always tempting for governments to protect incumbents have strong relationships with politicians and scream about 'sovereign risks' or lost jobs and wealth. Ironically, many objectors claim that increasingly powerful consumers are, in fact, vulnerable to these voracious disrupters. The extraordinary irony is that new digital applications are often designed to replace onerous and ineffective government regulation.

Even in traditional industries like retail, the loud voice of vested interest appears not just to stop innovation, but to prevent adaption to these disruptions. Online disrupters are accused of destroying retail strips, avoiding tax and killing jobs. It gets worse, because retail strips need to be able to adapt quickly to the change. Marcus Westbury points out in *Creating Cities* that something as simple as dated planning and property laws can hold back adaptation, innovation and entrepreneurship necessary to respond to this rapid change. His simple point is that in many cities, fast deteriorating high streets are natural 'incubators' for business development and innovation, but rental terms and conditions stem from an era when traditional bricks and mortar retail dominated activities on those streets. By creating new approaches for shorter term, lower cost, less regulated access to space, new incubation space can emerge in unexpected places.

The media sector demonstrates just how quickly we need to embrace this deregulation agenda. Australian regional TV stations are in serious decline as larger metropolitan based competitors stream content into the regions that has been sold at exorbitant prices to the regional players. In the absence of rapid deregulation, regional TV is in deep trouble. But worse, the natural adaptation of all media to cover voice, video and online will be stymied. It seems that this privilege is only bestowed on our public broadcaster, the ABC. Without deregulation, many Australians will miss the benefits of the fast evolving media landscape, offering extraordinary diversity of content and channels.

Governments at all levels need to develop and implement broad-ranging reforms to enable the digital economy and the benefits it offers. It is true that new business models may require adaptation of our tax policy, consumer protection and other areas of regulation. But a bias to deregulate is the right instinct. Imposing red tape to pander to vested interests ultimately puts jobs and prosperity at risk.

Every government agency from ASIC to the Department of Agriculture needs to look closely at how digital disruption can be supported by less regulation and better outcomes.

Enabling digital infrastructure

Much of the digital transformation we need across every aspect of industry and communities requires good infrastructure. The NBN debate between the idealists (wanting the perfect network straight away) and the pragmatists (wanting improvements quickly) has missed the real point. The role of government is to facilitate competition and innovation in the provision of digital infrastructure, and the NBN is just one important tool in that toolkit.

Competition is now unfolding at pace, and with it, new network capabilities. Nowhere is this clearer than regional Australia. Having laboured with Telstra's monopoly on fixed line networks for decades, regulatory and technology innovations are creating genuine competition.

Just as the NBN is rolling out fibre, towers and satellite into rural Australia, commercial providers are rapidly improving their mobile networks with 4G and lower frequencies freed up by government policy changes. This is increasing the reach and capacity of commercial networks. Many users are starting to see unprecedented choice, speeds and affordability. Some users, who recently only had access to dial-up speed through the failed 'interim satellite solution', can now access the NBN high speed satellite, Telstra 4GX and Optus 4G Plus. Spoilt for choice, many are struggling with finding the best option.

The government can do more to encourage this proliferation of choices, particularly in regional areas. For example, small providers of wireless network services struggle with affordable backhaul options (that is, moving data back from their towers to a data centre, typically in a city or major centre). By ensuring smaller network players get access to affordable backhaul, remote regions have the potential for high speed, affordable internet without overwhelming NBN satellite with finite capacity.

As we flood more and more of Australia with high speed data services, relatively remote industries like agriculture and mining can make better use of emerging technologies. Agriculture offers enormous potential for collecting and using large datasets, whether from weather observations, field data (e.g. crop yields), animal data (e.g. milk flows from dairy cows) or soil data (collected from soil moisture probes).

While the so-called 'internet of things' gains momentum, governments will also play a role in sensing and opening up data from public infrastructure and elsewhere. The most obvious example of this is in transport infrastructure, where improved data has the potential to reduce congestion, better prioritise investment and drive maintenance budgets.

Supporting commercialisation and skill development

Many of the biggest technology breakthroughs in recent world history have started as government driven research projects, including GPS, the internet and mapping the human genome. Typically, government fails in commercialisation where it often succeeds in providing more fundamental research.

At the same time, in Australia the private sector has been largely unsuccessful in commercialising quality research. There is a strong case for facilitating the pathway to commercialisation for digital technologies across a large range of industries, at least in the short term. The UK Catapult programme, as well as the Federal government's Growth Centres, is designed to support a renewed focus on commercialisation. In sectors that include agriculture, mining services and advanced manufacturing digital technologies are already having large impacts, and will continue to in the future.

Beyond this, there is much government can do to facilitate strengthened commercialisation. In particular, approval processes can be streamlined and accelerated to get new products to market quickly where approval is required (e.g. in the health sector). University academics and researchers can be rewarded for successful commercialisation of their research. Government procurement criteria can extend to include innovative new models and services exploiting digital technologies.

The government's focus on 'STEM' skill development is also crucial.

As waves of tech savvy young Australians look for opportunities to make their mark and build a business, digital government should be seen as a great opportunity. Most digital entrepreneurs are quick to point out that while commercial skills are important to commercialisation, technical and engineering skills are also crucial. There is no real shortage of ideas in the digital world – winners typically just execute better, and that often means elegant technical solutions.

The government can play a role in building private sector capabilities by changing its approach to procurement. As this monograph has pointed out, many problems faced by government can be solved through digitisation, but ideas will need to come from outside the private sector. Indeed, many big bureaucratic private sector organisations have used service providers to increase their pace of innovation.[60] Establishing a 'digital marketplace' is a big step in the right direction, so long as this is a marketplace for clever ideas that solve real problems, not just a procurement process.

Financing disruptive commercialisation of ideas is also central to accelerating the digital economy. Crowd-funding and employee share options are important tools and government needs to provide the right regulatory framework.

Setting digital standards across the economy

In some cases, it also makes sense for government to play a role in standard setting, to enable the rapid development of new digital applications using common standards.

The first and most obvious example of this, discussed above, is in the establishment of open standards for government. This can be as simple as the document standards that governments use. As a frustrated small UK business person – reliant on access to government information – recently put it: "I have almost no problems communicating with the outside world... except when it comes to government."[61]

These standards need to include software interoperability, data formats as well as document formats. For instance, accounting software needs to be able to interact with tax office data seamlessly, but that requires standard data formats as well as software interoperability. Central to this is use of simple APIs (application programme interface) to allow developers to access government data.

In some cases, standard setting needs to extend beyond direct government services to the digital economy. The number of devices that connect to the internet is exploding, requiring an expanding number of 'IP addresses'. Whether it is watches, weather stations, fridges, cars or air-conditioners, Gartner estimates that the number of devices attached to the internet reached almost 5 billion in 2015, and will reach 25 billion by 2020.[62] Government will be part of this, with applications like street lighting and traffic sensing. All of this has meant that we are close to running out of IP addresses for items attached to the internet, requiring a new standard called IPv6. This will provide a massive increase to the number of available addresses. Government can encourage standards like IPv6, by using them itself and by encouraging their use.

6

DIGITISING GOVERNMENT WITH URGENCY AND PURPOSE

- To build support for a broad-ranging and aggressive digital strategy, we need a focus on immediate benefits for citizens and governments
- Longer term benefits will flow from empowering citizens and customers to accelerate Australia's reform agenda
- To deliver these outcomes, government technology strategies need to be modular and agile
- Each department and agency should develop digital strategies, but highly skilled teams need to span across government and governments
- Success means bringing Australians on the journey – engaged citizens are central to the solution

The reach and benefits of digital government extend well beyond government websites replacing paper form filling. Digital government offers the potential for lower costs and taxes, better services, less onerous regulation and an economy embracing far reaching innovation and productivity. However, government needs to approach the task with the same energy and focus as the private sector has in recent years.

Each area of government needs to get moving on a journey that will start with simpler compliance and streamlining initiatives, and should extend quickly to much more profound reforms using all the levers of Government

2.0. The momentum for change must come from the top. Each area of government must embrace a broad-reaching programme that includes initiatives specific to each department, as well as initiatives that cross departments and even governments. Elected parliamentarians will need to sell the benefits of these programmes at every opportunity.

Probably the biggest barrier to success in these initiatives is in finding the unique mix of skills necessary to realise the opportunities. Governments need to attract and develop their capabilities. Calculated risk taking and short term failures should be encouraged, and shouldn't be 'career limiting'.

Realising immediate benefits: User-focused services, compliance and efficiencies

The most obvious short term initiative that can deliver immediate savings for government is to rapidly digitise the highest frequency transactions with government. As well as immediate benefits of strengthening more efficient channels, this will drive improved compliance and better targeting of big government spending programmes (e.g in health, welfare and general procurement) and taxation. As we saw earlier, across tax, health and welfare there are significant opportunities through compliance with existing legislation and regulation. In addition, better targeting spending initiatives based on integrated datasets offer the potential to improve the impact of major government initiatives.

As part of this strategy, targets for digital usage are important. Denmark set a target of 80% by 2015, and Australia should adopt a similar target for 2020. Digital by default, and the digitisation of all service lines are sensible aspirations, but the path to that aspiration needs to be carefully prioritised.

This will mean establishing projects that extend across all areas of government. From the point of view of the customer or citizen, 'myGov' (and the Australian Business Register) is a good starting point for this to happen,[63] but it needs to extend much further. Portals, whilst helpful, went out as the main entry point to the internet with the first tech wreck. Voluntary user controlled digital identities are very powerful part of 'myGov' and similar initiatives. We need to prioritise a single user controlled digital identity across all levels of government, as is happening in other countries, but with a sharp focus on privacy user control, and avoiding compulsion.

As Kathryn Campbell, the Secretary of the Department of Human Services points out:

> Particularly in the digital space, I think it would be disappointing if a customer who lived in one jurisdiction had their myGov password and their myGov login and then had to have another password and another login, and then if they were to move interstate, they then had to get a further login and further password.[64]

The UK has pioneered minimising rework for users across departments and organisations. When someone dies, 'Tell Us Once' carries all the relevant data across 44 different areas of government, including the UK's tax office (HMRC), the passport office, their Driver and Vehicle Licensing Agency, the Department for Work and Pensions and even local councils. In addition to this, also informs banks and other financial institutions.[65]

Capturing longer term benefits: Empowering Australians to drive tough reforms

Quickly finding savings and service opportunities will provide the political and financial capital to begin enabling much more profound reforms. Rather than deploying Government 2.0 initiatives broadly, it is more important to pick strategic areas for sharp focus. For instance, if we believe that greater contestability in the provision of health services – GPs, specialists, hospitals and allied health practitioners – offers big benefits, then this needs to be an area of focus. Customer ratings, objectively analysed government data, independent surveys, open data systems and data provision for new service models all offer the potential to shift power to the customer.

Central to this will be websites and applications – typically developed by third parties – to allow citizens and customers to make better choices across public services.

Sharpening the focus of government strategies also means realigning key digital initiatives and engaging outside skills. For instance, hackathons need to be made strategic. If healthcare is a priority data needs to be made accessible and hackathons (like Govhack) should be focused on these areas, and the specific problems government is seeing to solve.

This reform agenda, needs to reflect greater transparency and accountability for government spending. Open access to detailed information, with benchmarks where possible, needs to be part of an ongoing programme.

Reshaping our technology strategy: Prioritising modular, integrated apps

Successful digital government requires a technology strategy which is fast moving, sharply prioritised and delivers regular outcomes.

One of the most significant challenges faced by the Federal Government is the dreadful state of many of its systems, particularly the DHS systems. The systems date back from 1983, and include more than 350 components, while processing more than 50 million transactions each day. Much of the data initially entered through web based interfaces needs to be manually re-entered into the system. Layers of business rules, processes and policy changes built up over the past three decades have made it extremely complex, inflexible and costly to maintain.[66]

Clearly, these systems need to be progressively replaced, and the Government has already committed to a $1 billion project to do this.[67] The success of this project depends on moving away from the 'waterfall approach' to agile software development wherever possible. Doing so is the equivalent to switching from trench warfare to guerrilla warfare – a massive culture change for government, service providers and political leaders. In practice, it means breaking the project into a series of small modules prioritised based on where the benefits and impacts are greatest.

For instance, developing modules that allow simpler cross-checking with other databases – such as immigration, the ATO or even databases held by local and state governments – can be done quickly and cheaply rather than waiting for the new software platform to be developed.

There is also no doubt that the overhaul of the system will be aided by simplification and streamlining of welfare and health programmes, including the recommendations of the McClure review[68] and a series of health system reviews.[69]

Success will ultimately mean that the new applications and systems keep users in the digital channel from beginning to end, using simple, well tested (and quickly adapted) user interfaces. Where possible, forms should be pre-filled with data from across government systems.[70] With rapid improvements in online experiences outside of government, customers are increasingly demanding and impatient.[71] Mobile applications are an essential part of the solution – as we have seen in Scandinavian countries where citizens can pay their tax by SMS, for example.

Organising to support integrated strategies across government and governments

To support focused technology strategy, governments need integrated teams with leading edge skills. This means teams that work across all government departments, and who can engage effectively with other governments and the private sector. It also means that every government department and agency needs to be part of a much broader digital strategy. The Federal government's Digital Transformation Office is a big step in the right direction, although over time it will need to have clear mandates to shape a broad range of digital projects, including the Government 2.0 projects outlined in earlier chapters.

For instance, many past attempts to eliminate fraud abuse and errors have failed and not just in Australia.[72] To avoid past failures, these teams require a unique combination of IT skills, 'big data' experience, commercial acumen and a sharp focus which typically eludes government projects.

Compliance work like this requires teams with very strong analytical skills, and initially those skills should be developed and managed centrally. New York has successfully pioneered this approach, with the 'Mayor's Office of Data Analytics' (MODA) initiated by Michael Bloomberg.[73] New York, like most cities, was awash with data, but the data was providing little value for lack of necessary analytical skills. MODA filled that gap.

These teams need to rapidly form focused hypotheses about where to focus their efforts, linking various databases to quickly gather facts on non-compliance and poorly targeted spending. Poorly integrated government systems are not a barrier to skilled teams – they are able to obtain and link datasets to test their hypotheses, and form new ones. Effective teams need to be agile and focused on identifying waste.[74]

Similarly, highly capable teams need to focus on the best service and efficiency opportunities. Too much time and money can be wasted on areas that are not a strategic priority for the government. Whether it is in healthcare web interfaces or passport applications, these highly capable teams need to be deployed to the most impactful projects.

In addition to the skills required, government teams need the authority to access data across government. This is far more challenging than it should be. The NSW government has sought to solve this with new legislation requiring departments and agencies to provide data access to its data analytics centre – an initiative worthy of consideration across all Australian governments.

Engaging with Australians to make this happen

To realise the full potential of digital government, the Australian public needs to be engaged.

For starters, awareness and education are critical, and this will mean having 'educators' who can shift people online and help them to stay there. Customer service people who traditionally have just dealt with face to face or telephone interactions need to help people move online. This is increasingly challenging as the population continues to age. The Danish solution to this has been to develop 'digital ambassadors' – citizens and public servants, with supporting tools, who can help others to begin using digital government applications.[75]

Online integration also needs to be supported by bricks and mortar integration. The success of the NSW government with Service NSW is a good example of the level of real world integration required. To support this level of integration, it will be essential to train personnel with customer service backgrounds to become digital customer representatives at shopfronts.[76]

Increasingly, as governments move to 'digital first' strategies,[77] they will also need to shift to opt-out options for digital initiatives. For instance, the Federal electronic health records are now shifting to opt-out, meaning that all citizens will have a transferrable record unless they specifically ask not to have it.

Central to bringing Australians on this journey is the need to deal with privacy concerns and to maintain the trust of citizens. Whilst identity cards like the ill-fated 'Australia Card' have struggled to gain popular support,[78] modern approaches using personally controlled digital identities are very different. The success of Facebook and other social media and search engines in accessing unprecedented amounts of personal information tells us that customers will allow others to collate personal information if they have sufficient trust in privacy and security protocols, and there are real benefits in doing so.

To build trust, it is important to allow citizens to control their information if they choose to and to be very clear about how information will be used. Subject to that, a major backlash is unlikely. The UK government has gone one step further by offering the option of an online verification and identity assurance service, through third party providers.[79] So far, nine companies are included in the service, and citizens can choose between these companies.[80]

An important aspect of bringing citizens along with a strong digital government agenda is bridging the digital divide. Chapter 5 provided an overview of some of the network access issues involved, but online literacy is equally important. Broadband internet penetration and smart phone use in Australia is in line with or ahead of other OECD countries, although it falls sharply for Australians over the age of 65. We also know that income, education and region play a role in determining an individual's digital literacy.

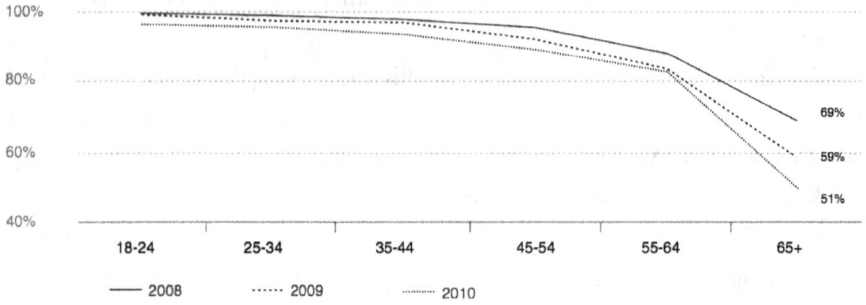

It is also clear that as the quality of online services improve, the usage increases. The reality is that some older Australians will never use applications or websites, but usage can be encouraged by the digital ambassadors and high quality online channels.

7

CONCLUSION

As the mining investment boom comes to a close, and Australia searches for the next big sources of growth to fuel the economy, innovations across all areas of the economy are desperately needed. Nowhere is that more important than government itself. More efficient government providing better targeted programmes and services should be a top priority for all governments and bureaucrats.

Digitisation of all aspects of government offers enormous potential to deliver better government at less cost. Less intrusive regulation, more accountability to communities and citizens and better use of taxpayers' money are all achievable.

Success will require every part of every government to understand the opportunity and embrace the challenge. The culture change required is enormous, but the prize makes it worthwhile.

REFERENCES

1 Robert Menzies, 'Democracy and Management', William Queale Memorial Lecture, Adelaide, 22 October 1954. Reprinted in *Robert Gordon Menzies, Speech is of Time,* Cassell & Company Ltd, London, pp. 193-208.

2 Avik Roy, 'Obama's website is crashing because it doesn't want you to know how costly its plans are', *Forbes magazine*, 14 October 2013.

3 William T Woods et al., 'HEALTHCARE.GOV: Ineffective Planning and Oversight Practices Underscore the Need for Improved Contract Management', United States Government Accountability Office, 30 July 2014.

4 Robert Pear et al., 'From the Start, Signs of Trouble at Health Portal', New York Times, October 13, 2013.

5 'Closing the $2.4 billion public sector productivity gap', EY Australian Productivity Pulse, 29 October 2013.

6 Mark Coultan, 'Mike Baird's fix for budgets: GST of 15pc', The Australian, 21 July 2015.

7 Mancur Olson, The Rise and Decline of Nations: Economic Growth, Stagflation, and Social Rigidities (New Haven: Yale University Press, 1982), pp. 166-170.

8 Amitabh Pal, 'John Kenneth Galbraith Interview', The Progressive, 13 April 2000, accessed 9 March 2015.

9 See more at http://www.progressive.org/mag_amitpalgalbraith#sthash.FpQRm9H8.dpuf

10 For example, see Paul Kelly, 'Broken system can't fix nation's problems', The Australian, 19 March 2015.

11 'Performance Audit Management of Smart Centres' Centrelink Telephone Services', The Auditor-General, ANAO Report No.37, 2014-15, at 37ff.

12 'Interacting with Government: Australia's Use and Satisfaction with e-Government Services', Australian Government Information Office (2011), p 19.

13 Gerard du Toit and Maureen Burns, *Customer Loyalty in Retail Banking:* Global Edition 2014, Bain and Company, 2015.

14 Roy Morgan Research, State of the Nation Australia, Report 19 - July 2014 (Melbourne: Roy Morgan Research, 2014)

15 'Consumer satisfaction with banks the highest in nearly two decades', Roy Morgan Research, Finding No 6103, 3 March 2015. http://www.roymorgan.com/findings/6103-consumer-satis-faction-with-banks-highest-in-nearly-two-decades-201503022255

16 Malcolm Edey, 'The Financial System in the Post-crisis Environment', Remarks to the Australian Centre for Financial Studies (ACFS) and Financial Services Institute of Australasia (Finsia) Leadership Luncheon Series, Melbourne, 22 March 2013. http://www.rba.gov.au/speeches/2013/sp-ag-220313.html

17 *Future of Fresh: Transforming the fresh food landscape over the next 20 years* (Woolworths Limited: 2014)

18 Stephen Easton, 'Kathryn Campbell: DHS service delivery reform a success, all things considered', *The Mandarin*, 21 August 2015.

19 Excludes information exchange between citizens and government.

20 *Deloitte Access Economics: Digital government transformation* (Commissioned by Adobe, 2015), p 1.

21 'Electronic Voting and Counting Around the World', The National Democratic Institute (NDI)

22 Vabariigi Valimiskomisjon, Statistics about Internet Voting in Estonia, European Parliament elections in 2014.

23 Electoral Commission NSW, iVote Reports, iVote SGE 2015 Specifications

24 Based on interviews with various management consultants.

25 DNP, or Do Not Pay, is operated by the Bureau of Fiscal Service.

26 Many other jurisdictions are moving in this direction e.g. Oregon in the United States, see Road User Charge Program: http://www.oregon.gov/ODOT/HWY/RUFPP/Pages/ruftf.aspx

27 UK Digital Efficiency Report, 2012. See www.gov.uk/government/publications/digital-efficiency-report

28 *Deloitte Access Economics: Digital government transformation* (Commissioned by Adobe, 2015), pp. 25-26.

29 David H. Autor 'Why Are There Still So Many Jobs? The History and Future of Workplace Automation', *The Journal of Economic Perspectives* (Vol. 29, No. 3, Summer 2015), pp 3-30.

30 National Archives of Australia Advisory Council, Annual Report 2012-13 (National Archives of Australia, 2013)

31 Australian Government, Department of Finance, Reports on Campaigning Advertising (2011-2015)

32 Australian Government, Department of Finance, 'Interacting with Government: Australia's Use and Satisfaction with e-Government Services' (Australian Government Information Office, 2011), Chapters 4, 7 and 10.

33 Australian Government, Department of Finance, 'Interacting with Government: Australia's Use and Satisfaction with e-Government Services' (Australian Government Information Office, 2011), Chapter 6.

34 *Deloitte Access Economics: Digital government transformation* (Commissioned by Adobe, 2015), p 37. Deloitte use the value of leisure time (estimated to be $10.61 per hour) rather than the value of work time, which is significantly higher.

35 'Street Bump App Locates Potholes, Gets Bossy with City Workers', *Huffington Post Technology*, 18 September 2012.

36 For example, Healthgrade.com rates doctors and dentists, ratemd.com rates doctors.

37 See, for example, Care Quality Commission: The Independent Regulator of Health and Social Care in England: http://www.cqc.org.uk/location/1-565923509

38 Claire Stewart, 'How Bureaucrat Pia Waugh is putting data front and centre into government', *Australian Financial Review*, 1 August 2015

39 Economists typically see competition as meaning there is real choice for customers, whereas contestability is when there is when there is a credible threat of competition, such as when a public sector utility will be outsourced to a third party provider if performance does not improve.

40 Gary L. Sturgess, 'Contestability in Public Services: An alternative to Outsourcing' (Australia and New Zealand School of Government, April 2015)

41 John Miklethwait and Adrian Wooldridge, *The Fourth Revolution: The Global Race to Reinvent the State*, (London: Penguin Press, 2014), Chapter 7.

42 Ste Davies, '10 Sensor Innovations Driving the Digital Health Revolution', *BIONIC.LY*, 6 March 2013.

43 For example, university lectures or customised student evaluation and support can be provided and regularly updated to parents and students online.

44 Parliament of Australia, The Senate, Research and Education: http://www.aph.gov.au/About_Parliament/Senate/Research_and_Education

45 Australian Bureau of Statistics, 4441.0-Voluntary Work , Australia, 2010, released 1 December 2011: http://www.abs.gov.au/AUSSTATS/abs@.nsf/Latestproducts/4441.0Main%20Features22010?opendocument

46 Hillary Sargent, 'Boston: 13,683 Fire Hydrants, 96 Inches of Snow', boston.com, 17 February 2015.

47 'How a Smartphone App Helps Ensure Tsunami Warnings', 15 April 2014:   http://www.accuweather.com/en/weather-news/smartphone-app-tsunami-warning/25426378

48 Phillip Hudson, Newspoll: Labor extends lead as entitlements scandal hurts coalition, *The Australian*, 9 August 2015.

49 Edmund Tadros and Markus Mannheim, 'Yes Please Minister: Labor Spends Billions on Advice', *Canberra Times*, 20 March 2012

50 Tim Binstead, 'Bupa goes after millionaire surgeons by publishing surgery prices', *Sydney Morning Herald*, 15 December 2015.

51 For example, see QRReader for iPhones.

52 'Encyclopedia: Definition of: Amara's law', *PC Magazine*, Retrieved 18 February 2015.

53 Olivia Nottebohm, James Manyika and Michael Chui, 'Guest column: Sizing the Internet economy in emerging countries', McKinsey & Company, 3 April 2012:

54 'The Connected Content II: How Digital Technology is Transforming the Australian Economy', An update to The Connected Continent 2011, Deloitte.

55 'Digital Disruption: Short Fuse, Big Bang?', Deloitte, September 2012.

56 James Manyika et al., 'Disruptive technologies: Advances that will transform life, business, and the global economy', McKinsey Global Institute, May 2013.

57 Timothy Aeppel, 'Be Calm, Robots Aren't About to Take Your Job, MIT Economist Says', The Wall Street Journal, 25 February 2015.

58 Chakravorti, Tunnard and Chaturvedi, 'Digital Planet: Readying for the Rise of the e-consumer' (Tuft University, 2014)

59 'Interacting with Government: Australia's Use and Satisfaction with e-Government Services', Australian Government Information Office (2011), Chapter 3, figures 4 and 5.

60 For instance, see Engel, Graff, Steffani, "Collaborative Supplier Innovation", ATKearney, 2014.

61 Linda Humphries, 'Setting open standards for government documents', Government Digital Service, Cabinet Office (UK), 4 December 2013: https://gds.blog.gov.uk/2013/12/04/setting-open-standards-for-government-documents/

62 'Gartner Says 4.9 Billion Connected "Things" Will Be in Use in 2015', Press Release, Barcelona, Spain, 11 November 2014: http://www.gartner.com/newsroom/id/2905717

63 MyGov can link to existing online accounts for Medicare, Centrelink, Child Support, the Department of Veterans' Affairs, the National Disability Insurance Scheme, the ATO and the Personally Controlled e-Health Record System.

64 Stephen Easton, 'Kathryn Campbell: DHS service delivery reform a success, all things considered', *The Mandarin*, 21 August 2015.

65 https://www.gov.uk/after-a-death/organisations-you-need-to-contact-and-tell-us-once

66 Hamish Barwick, 'Why the government is spending $1billion on Centrelink IT', *Computer World*, 10 April 2015

67 'Centrelink IT system replacement gets government go-ahead'. *Computer World*, 10 April 2015.

68 Australian Government, Department of Social Services, 'Review of Australia's Welfare System': https://www.dss.gov.au/review-of-australias-welfare-system

69 The Hon Sussan Ley, Minister for Health, 'Review of Medicare Benefits Schedule', 28 December 2015: https://www.health.gov.au/internet/ministers/publishing.nsf/Content/health-mediarel-yr2015-ley155.htm

70 For example, Denmark and Sweden presently make use of pre-filled tax returns. The Australian Taxation Office has introduced a similar service for Australian taxpayers. https://www.ato.gov.au/Media-centre/Speeches/Other/Tax-administration-transformation--Reinventing-the-ATO/

71 Capgemini, Digital Experience Optimisation (2014), see https://www.au.capgemini.com/resource-file-access/resource/pdf/14-07-02-dxo_brochure-final.pdf

72 'Performance Audit Medicare Compliance Audits - Department of Human Services', The Auditor-General Audit Report No.26 2013–1.

73 Eddie Copeland, *Big Data in the Big Apple,* 2015.

74 NSW Government: NSW ICT Strategy: News: Whole-of-Government Data Analytics Centre a Step Closer: https://www.finance.nsw.gov.au/ict/news/whole-government-data-analytics-centre-step-closer

75 Vital Rural Area (EU), Digital Ambassadors-Introduction to Digital Self-Service http://www.vitalruralarea.eu/broadband-digital-services/23-broadband-and-digital-services/114-digital-ambassadors-introduction-to-digital-self-service-dk

76 *Deloitte Access Economics: Digital government transformation* (Commissioned by Adobe, 2015)

77 Successfully applied in the UK: https://digital1st.co.uk/

78 Roy Jordan, 'Identity Cards and the Access Card', e-Brief, Bills and Digest Section, Parliamentary Library, Parliament of Australia (February 2006)

79 Introducing GOV.UK Verify, Cabinet Office and Government Digital Service (UK), 15 February 2016

80 Mark Say, 'GDS adds five and drops one from Verify', UKAuthority, Wednesday, 25 March 2015.

R. G. MENZIES ESSAYS OF IDEAS

Sir Robert Gordon Menzies kept a journal throughout his political life in which he would take notes of ideas, conversations and events.

The R. G. Menzies Essays of Ideas is published in the same spirit. It does not set out to be the last word on any given topic, merely a record of good ideas, articulately expressed, that may be enriched through further discussion.

If you would like to contribute to the debate online, or submit a contribution for future volumes, email: correspondence@menziesrc.org

Menzies Research Centre
Chairman: Tom Harley
Executive Director: Nick Cater
Deputy Director: Kay Gilchrist

PO Box 6091
Kingston ACT 2604
email: correspondence@menziesrc.org
www.menziesrc.org

R. G. MENZIES ESSAYS OF IDEAS

VOLUME 1

QUIET ACHIEVERS:
THE NEW ZEALAND PATH TO REFORM

OLIVER HARTWICH

Do today's politicians have the courage to make hard choices? Or has the furious pace of modern politics put an end to the age of reform?

In *Quiet Achievers*, Oliver Hartwich looks at New Zealand's record on spending, tax and welfare.

He discovers that while Australia has been avoiding difficult decisions, the New Zealanders have been silently forging ahead.

Oliver Hartwich is Executive Director of The New Zealand Initiative.

Series Editor: Nick Cater

"A perceptive analysis of the Key playbook" – Ruth Richardson

"A message that resonates across the Tasman" – Henry Ergas

Available from: www.connorcourt.com

R. G. MENZIES ESSAYS OF IDEAS

VOLUME 2

ON FAIRNESS

EDITED BY NICK CATER

Egalitarianism is a cherished Australian value. But in its modern guise of "fairness" it is corrupting political debate. *On Fairness* reveals how this fuzzy and contested concept leads governments astray. Liberty, rather than state control, provides the best path to a truly fair Australia.

Chapters include:
- The Moral High Ground – Nick Cater
- Envy Politics – Henry Ergas
- Fairness, Family and Freedom – Kelly O'Dwyer
- The Perils of Benevolence – Rebecca Weisser
- Tax, Regulation and Poverty – Alexander Scaife
- Conservative Social Justice – Iain Duncan Smith

Series Editor: Nick Cater

Available from: www.connorcourt.com

R. G. MENZIES ESSAYS OF IDEAS

VOLUME 3

GAME PLAN:
THE CASE FOR A NEW AUSTRALIAN GRAND STRATEGY

ROSS BABBAGE

The gravest duty of a government is not to balance the books. It is to protect its people.

But in an era of more challenging and complex threats, our greatest foe could be poor planning.

How can Australia avoid falling hostage to ad-hoc decisions, wasteful spending, bureaucratic inertia and fitful planning?

Game Plan argues for a new Grand Strategy – a blueprint to deter the next war, and, if forced to fight, to win.

Ross Babbage is a senior defence analyst and the head of Strategy International.

Series Editor: Nick Cater

Available from: www.connorcourt.com